I AM IMPORTANT
Poetry on the Bookcase
ANGEL-CLARE LINTON

i just wanna talk to someone. i just wanna be heard.

Poetry on the Bookcase

a poetry collection by angel-clare adiel linton

Linton Press

POETRY ON THE BOOKCASE
Copyright © 2023 by Angel-Clare Linton

All rights reserved. No part of this publication may be used in any form or fashion, such as being transmitted or reproduced electronically or physically / mechanically (i.e. recording, photocopying, or any information retrieval and storage system). The writer or publisher must grant written permission unless small portions of this publication are used in reference to critical articles or reviews.

All names used in this collection are from the poet's imagination.

For more information, please visit: www.lintonpress.ca

Cover design and edited by Angel-Clare Linton

ISBN: 978-1-7387049-5-8 (Paperback)
ISBN: 978-1-7387049-8-9 (PDF)
ISBN: 978-1-7387049-4-1 (eBook)

First edition: June 2023

10 9 8 7 6 5 4 3 2 1

TRIGGER WARNINGS

Poetry on the Bookcase is a poetry collection that discusses depression, anxiety, suicide & suicide ideation, self-harm (specifically cutting), & an abusive (romantic) relationship, &, in most cases, it goes into detail about such topics; thus, the themes discussed in this collection may be triggering to some readers. Reader discretion is advised.

PLAYLIST

Spotify Profile: angelclare_

Little Do You Know by Alex & Sierra

Hold On by Chord Overstreet

Insecurities by Damien

Happier by Ed Sheeran

How to Save a Life by The Fray

When You Lose Someone by James TW

All of Me by John Legend

Someone You Loved by Lewis Capaldi

Lost on You by Lewis Capaldi

Before You Go by Lewis Capaldi

Hold Me While You Wait - Recorded at Spotify Studio NYC by Lewis Capaldi

when the party's over - Recorded at Spotify Studio NYC by Lewis Capaldi

Shallow - BBC Radio 1 Live Lounge by Lewis Capaldi

1-800-273-8255 by Logic, feat. Alessia Cara & Khalid

The Search by NF

Change by NF

Time by NF

Hate Myself by NF

Lost in the Moment by NF, feat. Andreas Moss

July by Noah Cyrus

Dead and Cold by SadBoyProlific

Alone - slowed + reverb by SadBoyProlific

Dead and Cold - slowed + reverb by SadBoyProlific

Midnight Thoughts - slowed + reverb by SadBoyProlific

Elastic Heart by Sia

I'm Not Enough and I'm Sorry by Teqkoi, feat. Snow

You Broke My Heart Again by Teqkoi, feat. Aiko

Leave a Light On by Tom Walker

Unsteady by X Ambassadors

changes by XXXTENTACION

Jocelyn Flores by XXXTENTACION

Everybody Dies In Their Nightmares by XXXTENTACION

«Fear not, for I *am* with you; Be not dismayed, for I *am* your God. I will strengthen you, Yes, I will help you, I will uphold you with My righteous right hand.'»
Isaiah 41:10 NKJV

TABLE OF CONTENTS

14	shelf one - the night watcher
66	shelf two - the poisonous antidote
112	shelf three - illusions of talk therapy
126	about the writer

shelf one

the night watcher

I'm not safe & don't know if I'll ever be safe.

radio silence

In the movies, silence is the perfect family home.

It's the small table in the middle of the kitchen
with four chairs around the round table.
     The tables
          & chairs
              & cutlery
                   & radio
are pastel pink & blue.

The house has four stories
with a silver elevator
next to the echoing wooden stairs.
It's the type of house to be in a home magazine
you would skim through
as you shop for the ideal dark brown rug,
& the red & green jealousy in the form of liquid goo
creeps inside you like a vicious lion
hunting its prey.

     You've always wanted a house like that
     but could never afford it

unless you sell your kidney,
right arm, & maybe your left leg, too.
The house constantly has white sunlight
echoing off the light brown & white walls.
There are somehow
    n e v e r
any toys, clothes, & notebooks
with white or cream pages spilling out
& spoons that never seem to be enough
    s c a t t e r e d
throughout the house,
    d e s p i t e
having two tiny dolls
sitting on the pure white couch
in the living room before their mother yells
at them to get off & to "go to your room."

In the movies, silence is seemingly
the perfect family home

    in a suburban neighbourhood
    at the end of a cul-de-sac
    where many young families reside

as white-collar crimes
coated in light grey covers the neighbourhood,
but the figurine-like people pretend
they're the perfect neighbourhood.

The radio plays static like an off-tune mother
as she insists on singing her favourite song
at the top of her lungs
because it makes her happy. But no one listens
or bothers to fix her singing, just like the radio.

The dolls sit at the table
as their parents cook dinner.

The mom laughs, throwing
her dark brown hair back,
& the dad lets out a low, deep laugh
that rumbles the earth.

The dolls talk about faeries
magic kingdoms & how to travel
to an alternate dimension.

I am that radio.

life is in the blood,

but similar to a waterfall sparkling at night, I want it to
        s
           l
               o
                   w
                       l
                           y
come out from the self-harm cut on my left arm
when the night has long since consumed the city
in a dark blue coating with sparkling neon white stars
& a moon that hears people's crying whispers.

Even though red monsters roam the streets
while the glistening moon shines
in the middle of the night
as the city's covered in dark blue
(or whenever it's dark blue outside),
I can watch the shimmering city lights
as I sit on a dark green hill.
        I can stare at the freckled moon
        & whisper sweet nothings
        like it's my home.

Birds ain't flocking & loitering
like high schoolers
during their lunch break
while a car or two zooms past, desperate
to arrive home only to fall asleep
in their cloud-shaped bed.

My breaths are nearly transparent white clouds
that quickly disappear in the sky.

Someone can easily kidnap me
as the stars continue to shimmer
alongside the moon.

Life is in the blood,
but I want the dark red waterfall to
      o
           o
                z
                     e
out of my arm as if it's desperate
to escape the house fire
that quickly consumes the home
while the night prolongs the darkness,
keeping a half-moon shining in the sky
when it's early enough for the majority
of people to enter the streets.

The fluorescent white light

bounces off the bathroom walls upstairs
as if desperate to watch the air sting
the wound like fists
smashing the walls
in an abandoned building.

The night air dances with the full moon
        while
transparent silence bounces outside.

the cuts & brows

There were more fresh cuts when I was 18.
The fresh air would constantly sting the scars,
tingling my body, whispering for me to do it more
so I could fight off the black weights
& dark blue ocean sitting on my chest.

The blood would slowly pour out
like tears from someone
who just went through a breakup.

The blood would nearly curd as it would escape
from my torn skin like someone running
a track & field race.

I would control the flow of life
as I would quickly clean it up
before I would do it again
as the adrenaline would rush throughout my body
like being in a waterpark for the first time.

the black kiss of the moonlight

was there the night before
my most recent suicide attempt.

The city was echoing in quietness.

The street lights twinkled
like it was someone's 18th birthday.

Stars weren't littered in the dark blue sky.

The black kiss of the moonlight
as it played with the stars squeezed
its way into my pinkish-grey brain,
coating it in matte black.

The frosty blue cold consumed my body,
& begged me to feel the coldness of the air.

When the sun was shimmering
the day of my attempt,
I couldn't tell my counsellor
how I would keep myself safe.

But then, as the sun dimmed,
the heaviness in my chest,
like weights in an apartment's community gym,
was still there from counselling.

Should I have told him

I was gonna attempt suicide?

Should I have made a plan with him?

Did I make a mistake?

I wanted to be consumed in the darkness
& be as beautiful as the vibrant lights in the night.

the green bombs

predominantly litter my thighs.

My thighs extend like a large bouncy ball
people would find in a grocery store.

I don't know why my ex adored them
like people doting on newborn babies.

The bombs are dead
like the grass turning light brown
as the sun hammers onto the grass
as it cries out, "We need water."

But then the bombs suddenly explode,
killing the invisible people
& leaving the person placing the bomb
eternally in critical condition.

the nervous system: our brain

is mainly made up of neurons (a.k.a nerve cells).
Similar to a parent taking care of their children,
they're responsible for obtaining sensory input
from the outside world. They establish
or define who we are &, like a stay-at-home parent,
do far more than what many people think.

Neurons are comprised of your thoughts,
memories, emotions, & hunger.
They're like the matte black building blocks
of depression.

Your thoughts can be consumed by
I ain't good enough,
I ain't smart enough,
&
I ain't worthy enough.

Some nights, when I'm lying in my bed,
wrapped up under the pink covers
that seemingly aren't enough to keep me warm,
this collection ain't good enough,

& I shouldn't continue with my career,
wiggles in my mind
like a worm coming out
when it rains during the spring, desperate
to get some sort of interaction.

Maybe I should be someone else.

    Your memories are like homemade videos,
which sometimes automatically play on repeat
during the night. Like videos, there are time jumps,
& depending on the night, you cry into your pillow
as you wonder,

Why can't I remember my life?

What did I eat for breakfast on Saturday?

What day does school start again?

What day is it today again?

    Emotions cast through your body
like white liquid trying to keep you alive.
It's like the approximate 60% water
floating throughout your body like fish bait
floating in the ocean.

For me, there's sometimes, dark blue sand
that somehow consumes my back,
sucking me into its hot hug
like a mother comforting her child
after being bullied at school.

    Emotion's white liquid dances into your brain,
         convincing you to not eat
      because *eating's just a waste of time.*

      Hunger is basically invisible until something
            itches it, demanding
      it to knock on Stomach's door, insisting
              it's hungry.

When the itch begins to yell,
it forces my body to get up,
nearly tripping over its own weight,
& make food to satisfy my pink stomach.

People's brains are mainly made up of neurons,
& similar to a parent taking care of their child,
they're responsible for obtaining sensory input
from the outside world. They establish
or define who we are &, like a stay-at-home parent,
do far more than what many people think.

suicide

In English class, the sun shimmered
through the small, square windows of the classroom.
It bounced off the tables & in people's eyes.
My body was illuminated in frosty blue,
which consumed my body in its coldness.
A black monster named Suicide
crawled at the back of my mind
& whispered black roses & deep brown daisies
in my yellow, sunflower ears.

My body squirmed in my seat,
wanting me to be in my soft, home.

IByte danced on my laptop.

My digital notes were in the background.

The prof's voice drowned
my subconscious listening in the beach's ocean.

I texted my friend about "the least impactful suicide."

     I would bleed out in the bathroom
       as the light would fade
      from my dark brown eyes
    before people would have the opportunity
       to celebrate my birthday.

I don't think I should tell her whenever

     I feel suicidal.

Maybe I should keep that part of my life private.

I don't think people really care about me.

Then there was a dark blue feeling,
& it sat like a lonely ball
in the corner of the classroom
after his classmates rejected him
because "he was too shy."
The feeling consumed my body
& ate me like a starving young adult male
after coming home from his labour-intensive job.

Suicide would turn me dark blue,
which would cause people to stare
at me like an alien from Mars.

"All forms of suicide are dangerous,"

she texted me as if I was in immediate danger.

Maybe I shouldn't have told her I was suicidal.

mercury

is thick & d red & follows me
like a child learning to walk.

It's large, like the galaxy,
& it dances & shimmers while people stargaze.

                Bumpy

                    Alone

Lost in the system.

I'm a failed science experiment.

    Small

            Disappearing

                    Gone

the overdose on 9th street

The psychiatrist who prescribed me antidepressants
the second time I was detained
was of an average height with short, black hair.
He was skinny with black, shiny shoes
that slightly shimmered in the hospital room's lighting.

When I was on it,
>my hunger decreased,
>like the value of a company
>in the stock market.

>I nearly threw up like a pregnant woman
>in the middle of the night.

>Whenever my body wasn't standing,
>it was as if I was floating with the clouds
>& inches away from escaping Earth.

I stopped being on antidepressants
despite the bottle still being filled
with white dots that move
whenever the bottle moves.

Maybe I wasn't on them long enough.
                        Maybe I should go back on them.
But what if I were to overdose on them?
                    I can just overdose on them now.
It's not like anyone would miss me,
                        care, or notice I'm gone.
              Right?

The urge to swallow the pills
like eating candy scratches
my brain like nails scratching my arms
while outside on a bright yellow day.

I don't think I'm safe enough to keep those pills.

the hospital in the suburban city

was like the sun, except it was white.

I

A short woman with black hair came into the room
while the cops were outside
as they wrote on their white pages with blank ink.

I.I

"What's your marital status?"
I dryly laughed. "Single."

I.II

The cops left at around this time.

I was alone like a cat abandoned by its owner
on the streets before wandering in an alleyway.

II

He was a medical doctor
of average height with black hair & brown eyes.

I was sitting on the soft blue hospital-like bed.

He crossed one leg over the other
as he sat opposite me
in his dark grey or black pants
with (I think) his white coat.

While he checked my heart rate,
the cold stethoscope
was trying to find its home.
It tickled, and I chuckled.

He was satisfied and left.

III

The psychiatrist of average height
with short, black hair opened the door
& greeted me with the type of smile
he would give to other patients.

"Can I sit?" he asked
as if he wanted me to feel in control of something.

I shrugged, & he sat down
before we talked as if he was my therapist.

"I don't remember the name of the antidepressants."

        "Was it [name I still don't remember]?"

"Yes! That was it."

                    "I would have been surprised if it wasn't."

                          IV

The city was quiet.
                    The streets were nearly empty.
It was almost the next day.

I got a slightly tinted white paper
with my prescription written in the blanks
like a fill-in-the-blank game for young children.

                        IV.I

I got into the dark yellow fish tank
the hospital paid for
& arrived home
as if I just came back from a concert.

**the midnight air
dances with the full moon**

Sleep is in the shape of a white cloud
drawn by children. It plays soft music
as I sit on my bed with my laptop on my lap
and watch uPrime videos while writing.

Is life even worth living?

Sleep is desperate for me to crawl into its arms
as it's ready to rock me to sleep
like a mother putting her child to bed at 8 p.m.
It wants me to drift off into a deep slumber
like a father after he comes home from work,
too sleepy to even eat.

I don't want to embrace the beauty of sleep.

Suicide dances around my head
like a needle in a glass bottle
as someone ruthlessly shakes it
while the disco ball shakes
as it casts rainbows in the world,

reminding them of *that* promise.

It's like I'm on a freshly shaven ice rink
without any skates as Suicide pushes me around
the rink while its body rubs off on me,
staining me with black dots scattered around my body
as if I was coming home from painting a house.

No one cares about me.

Should I just kill myself?

It's as if I'm a marionette sitting in a light brown box
as someone from above controls me
with invisible strings while polka dots sit
in bed-like chairs sit with a crime-like grin
as my lifeless body flops around
like an upset child throwing a temper tantrum.

Suicide dances around my head
like a needle in a glass bottle
as someone ruthlessly shakes it
while the disco ball shakes
as it casts rainbows in the world,
reminding them of *that* promise.

It dances around my head
while Sleep is still in the shape of a white cloud
drawn by children as it continues to play soft music.

suicide is

the light blue skies. The sun on the opposite side of the world casts dark orange & purple sunsets. TV shows on a laptop. A quiet house made to feel like a home. The decline of the economy.

the darkness with the half moon in the middle of the day. A dark house. Someone breaking in. Being murdered. Not expecting to die as you take your final white breath.

the trees swaying in nature. The calmness as the home is scattered with violence. The yellow night light in the corner of the bedroom. Fresh food in the fridge. The bird sits on a tree branch as a dark grey storm thrusts around it.

the emptiness sitting where the stomach should be. The black skies. The light in the house. A disappearing person as no one notices. No one cares.

suicide.

counselling

After my first suicide attempt,
it was like I was a 6-year-old child
forced to come with my mother
to the grocery store because "no one's home"
to take care of me.

Then it was as if I broke away from the silver,
dirty chains that wrapped around my body,
holding me down on the muddy,
silver ground in a room without windows.

Now it's like I'm walking to the grocery store
at 7 in the morning with a sunshine smile,
only to come out of the store
with a grey-tinted face, dark blue ocean eyes,
an unconscious frown & a slight frown.

the darkness of the night consumes me.

But earlier this semester, I didn't have to speed walk
in the darkness, cutting through it
like a chainsaw through pieces of wood.
I didn't have to shove my way through its home,
fighting the silver, shiny, & spiky grounds
as if I was walking on block toys at home.

My dark blue thoughts

(You're worthless)

(You should die)

(No one would ever care about you)

would bounce around the inside of the bus,
demanding that I pay attention to it.

Earlier in the semester, a light
would be in the corner of my body, flickering.

The bus would force me to confront
what was behind my hidden smile,
like a teacher in secondary school
forcing me to do my homework
if I wanna pass their class.

A person down the street wears shorts
as if it's the middle of the summer
in the Caribbean or France.
How ain't that person cold?

Because of my astigmatism,
the illumination of traffic lights & street lamps echo
into my eyes like the sudden shine of the sun
through my bedroom.

My breaths are clouds in the sky.

I can't wait to be home.

A line forms behind me.
There's another line forming to my right.

I get on the bus & pay.

I sit at the back of the bus.
Should I be sitting at the back of the bus?

A gust of wind plays with my slim statue

as I wait for the second bus at the station.

The wind whispers.

People are sparse.

The moon shines brighter than the sun.

Music beats in my white earphones.

I can't wait to get home.

The bus comes speeding along,
crashing at the bus stop
two & a half songs later.

The heat of the bus engulfs me.

the third suicide attempt

It was the 10th month on the 6th day in 2022.
    It should have been the perfect plan, like a wedding after a year & a day of consistent planning.
        I shouldn't have shouted my plan to him as if I was in the night air
            like someone desperate for help.
A psychiatrist & cop should have been there,
        but two male cops were forced to deal with me & the night sky.
      I thought they were only there to talk.
I got detained again
        under the mental health act
as if my life would be destroyed
           within the hour.
The even numbers are like a baby sibling
        following their eldest sibling.
Three suicide attempts.
      Maybe I should try again to make it even.
      How can people actually care about me?
    I got detained a little over two years apart.

Tears consumed my eyes,
        only to escape seconds later, defying my wants
like certain secondary students in school.
        I should have been talking to a psychiatrist.
I don't think I should have been detained.
                      I wasn't safe, was I?
He was just doing his job.
                    What if he doesn't care?
He was just doing his job.
        A psychiatrist & cop should have been there.

While staring out of the bus window
                like a woman in a romance movie,
I got an email from my counsellor
        while the music continued to echo in my ear.

            He was just doing his job.

It was as if the bus wasn't going fast enough,
        as if purposely wanting me to be late for class.
            I was biting the inside of my mouth
& the corner of my bottom lip.

He wanted to make sure I was okay.

        He just wanted to help me, right?

I shouldn't have used those services.

Look where that led me.

Maybe I shouldn't have let someone crawl
               into my body, wanting to heal my heart.

The cops were there rather than a psychiatrist
     with a cop in the distance like a substitute teacher
because the psych was too busy,
             like a teacher during the weekend
        after a Friday test on the previous two units.

My heart ever so slightly chipped away
                        as it continued to pump,
still trying to keep me alive
             as if my body was slowly shutting down
like the lights to the country's university campus.

No one cares.

It was as if I was trash that got taken out
                           earlier that day.

I shouldn't have agreed to those services.
               I should have killed myself.

       Maybe I should attempt again.

ive obviously failed at suicide.

Failure taunts me like a bully on the playground
during recess, egging the victim along
like a lawnmower driving on the concrete
before kissing the grass on a boiling summer's day.

It ain't the red monster lurking
at the end of the hallway
in the middle of the darkness, waiting
for its next victim as the sun
is scheduled to rise in the next hour & a half.
It doesn't sit in a dark brown chair
at the end of the hall like a mother
waiting for her child to come home. Instead,

Failure is the pastel pink Azalea
as it dances & twirls with the wind, laughing
like a young woman with her friends on the bus
to the beach.

When I failed at allowing the iron blood to burst
through my body like water
bursting through a beaver dam,

there would be this tiny, spiky twang in my chest,
& tears would threaten to spill out
whenever my mind chose to sit down & dwell
on the suicides that were just out of reach.

Some nights, my brain eggs me on
as it sits on a hard wooden chair
at the dining room table, yelling at me, forcing me
to stare at it in its eyes,
wanting me to see the holes
contained with nails & knives
sketched around its oval face.

Failure stares at me like a vampire thirsty for blood,
tempting me to follow it or be consumed
by its pure white fangs & black eyes.

Somewhere in my mind, there's a white paper
with light grey ink labelled
                    "Suicide Plan"
written at the top. It constantly
flaps around like a country's flag
at the parliament building.

The paper sometimes screams at me, insisting
that I use it like a bully
showing off on the playground during lunch
& comforting me with sunshine black words saying,
it's normal to always have me by your side.

The paper only contains bullets.

   Overdose.   Bleed out.
     An accident that couldn't have been avoided.

Meanwhile, Failure wants me to hold onto that paper
& be in her grasp & control like the villain.

Failure shrivels up, screeching
if the smell of orange fruitcake,
cheesecake, & flowers
in a warm house on a Saturday afternoon
as a mother bakes
with the rest of the members
of her baking club
consumes her nostrils.
But it only happens
whenever there's this scratch
behind her ear
whenever she thinks

she ain't needed.

Failure, who insists that her name is "far too harsh,"
whispers in my ears as I lay in my bed,
wrapped like a burrito as I watch uPrime videos
as they echo in my bedroom.

I wish she whispered sweet nothings
while laying beside me like a friend at a sleepover.
But she whispers, *how pathetic that life & death*
      don't want you, &
                where does that leave you?

On some nights, when my house shushes itself
before falling into a deep sleep
as quick as a father during the middle of the day
after waking up at 4 in the morning just for the vibes,
I curl up in my bed. White clouds float around
for three and a half seconds
before forcing their way into my mind; wondering,
          Were they really suicide attempts?
Can you really claim them as such?
            If they ain't a suicide attempt,
    what can I call them?

imposter?

    I don't know what to associate with "Imposter."
I don't know if he should be dressed in green or red
or have a white suit while sitting in the corner
of a hot pink bedroom. I don't know if he should
have a square face with a chiselled jaw
like those in romance movies
aimed at young adult women.
Or the ones with shirtless men on the cover
of adult women's romance books.

I've only ever seen him once or twice
while walking across the street. He tipped
his black hat towards me with a smile,
showcasing his dimples, which gained a smile
& a light chuckle from me
as we continued our separate ways
like a couple breaking up.

    I don't know what to associate with Imposter.
But maybe it can shapeshift
& is liquid goo that younger children
are sometimes fascinated with.

On a day when the schoolwork
ain't forcing me to swim in my home
or during a school night, the sentence
    People think I'm smarter than I actually am
wiggles in my mind like a baby dancing.
That phrase comes at me like a sudden basketball
hitting me in the face during P.E. class
as bright red Embarrassment smears
on my face like children egging
their neighbour's house on Halloween night.

People think I'm smarter than I actually am.
That phrase is always dressed
in a black & white ball gown dress,
& it dances on a disco dance floor like it's prom again.
That phrase has an oddly shaped wide grin
as if it wants to murder whoever wiggles in its pathway.

Loud music booms like a drummer
practicing before their second concert.
It vibrates in my brain
like a neighbour somewhere in the distance,
always playing loud music with a heavy base
that somehow you constantly hear echoing
to your house like a wave
on a beach as it captures a beach towel.

    I should have been asleep.

I think it's Imposter who forces the tangled sentence,
                Not because you're in university
& getting grades mean you're smart.

When the sun was still in the sky,
performing its own dance & evening performance,
I was sitting on the light brown couch
in one of the bedrooms of my house,
allowing my body to relax as if I had time to do so.

My magical words containing a galaxy
don't bleed out into the Internet,
ready to explode like a fairy in a forest
that blocks the sunlight.

Imposter tells me,
                "Nothing of value is in your name,"
&
                "You're a walking failure,
shining as bright as a red stop sign
                in the middle of the darkness
in a mid-sized town."

The night's half-moon illuminates in the sky,
serenading the twinkling stars.

I should be in a dark sleep
as my dreams drive in & out of my brain

like cars during rush hour,
as some of them drive into a drive-in movie theatre.
UPrime videos continue to play as I write in Scribble.

I think Imposter has been whispering
in my ears with black music notes in the B scale.
How can you possibly think

your writing is good enough?

You shouldn't even continue writing this collection.

You should quit while you're ahead.

I don't know if it's Imposter anymore.
I don't know if he's the one
who whispers, *Is life even worth fighting for?*
in the night air with fiery smoke tinted in its stars.

I don't know what Imposter looks like
& if he's the one that wandered into my life
like a random stranger knocking on my door
at 8:01 a.m. wanting to be my friend.

I ain't know if Imposter was the one
who insisted that I'm just an imposter (like him)
one night, only to disappear like an adult
skipping town in the middle of the night.

i remember seeing the sunset.

Yesterday, I was on campus, laughing
& playing card games with people
while the writing club was in full swing,
like a university graduation party
that started a little over two hours ago.

Someone from another club
popped her head in, joining us in the game
while continuing to laugh & eat chips & donuts,
which I later brought home.

Outside the room, the building was quiet,
oblivious to the spark of light & life
that happened in the room.

The designated time for the club ended,
but we continued to talk
as if we had been friends for four years.

"Hey, there's the sunset," I said
as we were sitting at the large tables
on the second floor.

Orange hues were playing in the skies,
& someone took a photo.

But then we left, disbanding like a boy band
that teen girls were head over heels
in love with ten years ago

The yellow colour radiant
that protected me from the thick blackness
in the room slowly faded as I speed-walked
to the bus stop while rap music
played in my ears,
hoping to keep the blackness

away from me.

Light pink energy escaped my body
as I sat on the bus, desperate for me to get home.

An itch was there, wishing I was there for longer,
wanting the light pink energy to radiate from me.

I didn't want the blackness
to climb on my body,
holding me to the floor like a prisoner.

I eventually shook it off & fell asleep,
only to be forced to drag my body
out of bed & interact with the world.

life is an interesting thing.

Suicide wasn't there, trying to control me
& have me in his slippery black grip
while trying to accomplish my daily schoolwork,
thinking that, at this point, I should get paid for it.

As I was wandering through my last year
of secondary school, I wanted to escape
into adulthood, envisioning I'd be galloping
on the outskirts of town,
slightly desperate to have that freedom.

But as adulthood slowly came,
freedom opened up, its arms
wide open, waiting for me to hug it
as if I hadn't seen it for a decade.
I embraced it, thinking my life
would be consumed in something magical
& vastly different from only seconds ago.

The feeling of something magical happening
as the clock struck midnight, like my dress
suddenly turning an icy pink, didn't come.

However, the pastel red, green,
& yellow ball called excitement took over
as if it wasted its entire life for this moment.

Suicide wasn't there, trying to control me
& have me in his slippery black grip
while trying to accomplish
my daily schoolwork, thinking that, at this point,
I should get paid for it.

Towards the end of grade 12, though,
this black *thing*
covered my chest, convincing me
that no one likes me & that

I should hurt myself.

I craved to be alone, consumed
with my thoughts & enjoying the time
I had with myself after being forced
to socialize in a world of extroverts.

I wasn't truly alone, though.

When I was 17 & couldn't wait to graduate,
I often cut my wrists.

The wounds were on my wrist,
desperate for people to see them

& ask if I was okay,
but I was afraid to tell them the truth.

Adulthood slowly passed
& three years later, at 21,
there was this feeling
that I'd been holding freedom's hand
for much longer than three years,
most likely because of User X.

the end of an era contains

the warm air as it cuddles me
while a light mist of pollution circles the skies.

It tussles around the leaves & bushes,
& the clouds cause the skies to be cotton candy.

It's the thick of summer,
& a mixture of strawberries, banana bread,

& other baked goods dance in the air,
trying to fend off the pollution.

My heart was dark grey,
trying to get back pink.

Should I reply now? I think
as my friend's message

pops up on my "phone."
Heaviness & Dread

linger in my mind.

Does that make me a bad friend?

Burden is always there, pestering me
like a bird that, for some reason,

never leaves me alone. The end of an era

wants me to greet it with a broad smile
that reaches my eyes while small yellow birds

fly around me as if protecting me
from zombies on people's lawns

as I walk down the road. But some days
(when I think I shouldn't be who I am),

I lock myself in my room
like voluntary solitary confinement

so that Burden doesn't repeat in my mind
like a song I recently discovered.

Trees swing with the hot wind
while I watch writing videos as I write.

The imagination is two-sided. One side's covered
in white, while the other's covered in black.

Depending on which side you get, you can

be screaming while walking down the street,

or walking with the clouds.
Or maybe you wake up screaming as you think
you're still in the haunted house

with the black curtains, thinking that the skeleton
is still crawling on the ceiling,

covered in black paint, wanting to eat you.
Or you're waking up, thinking,

I wish I could go back to sleep.

The end of an era contains the warm air
as it cuddles me with clouds
while a light mist of pollution circles the skies,
begging me to come with it.

shelf two

the poisonous antidote

What if he's after me? What if he wants to poison me?

i was a victim

when I was 18. As the world was shifting,
it was as if I was trapped in something
with a rose & red-tinted outlet, thanks to me.

I made the leap into my university years
like a baby walking for the first time.

                Some nights, when I cry in my bed
                    before falling asleep, this *thing*
                 somehow appears inside my body,
      exploring it like a diver exploring a new dive area.

He was the first tooth that came in
while I learned what the world around me was.

It began with seeing a white "stump" in the gums,
but then, as the "stump" grew bigger & bigger,
the baby started to constantly cry, agonizing
with the unwanted pain throughout the transition.

                That was me.

But then the baby got all their teeth in
& stopped crying.

I got all my "teeth" in 91.2501 days
& stopped crying like that baby.

User X would crawl into my mind,
scrambling my thoughts
& come out of my residence
telling me, "I've always
supported your poetry," despite
nearly turning off his ears
while I would talk about my writing
unless it benefited him.

Some days, as the weather flip-flops
like me deciding where to move to next,
a sneaky thought enters my mind,
slivering into every open hole.

The thought is muddled
& like noodles in a web.
I ain't know what to make of it.

You couldn't fix the relationship.
                      You should have worked harder.
My mind yells back,
                      But it wasn't my fault.

That has followed me
as I've attempted to maneuver
throughout the world tinted in grey.

His arms snuck into my mind as I slept,
playing around with my head,
scrambling my thoughts to give him a slightly
less grey-tinted view of himself,
trying his hardest to still appear
like the perfect & ideal boyfriend.

Why did I ever date him?

He threw his bright yellow ball at me,
expecting me to grab it
& take care of it for him
like a mother taking care of her minor child.

He then threw a piece of his brain,
demanding me to catch it,
keep it in my front pocket,
& feed it with light pink love
while not giving it back.

I kept his yellow ball
& the piece of his brain, watering it
like a plant & caring for it
like a newly born puppy
because he was my boyfriend,

& he said he was clingy
as if it was setting me up
into thinking it was normal (which worked).

When we met online in January 2020,
our floating messages floated
through the Internet outer space to each other
a few messages per day,
scattered throughout the day.

But then, as if there was a piece in his brain
that switched on March 15th, 2020
(the day I agreed to be his girlfriend)
& decided that "it was time,"
the floating messages from his side
would invade my screen with notifications
as if he was in a medical emergency.

A piece of my sanity got chipped away.

The flooded notification bar
would hurt my chest like a wrecking ball
bursting my heart, making it difficult
for me to breathe as if I was trapped underwater.

I held my head above the black water,
treading lightly as I spat out the water
as it tinted my mouth, trying to swivel
to my mind to tell me that

I ain't good enough
                                                            &

I should kill myself
               & that
                             no one would care when I'm gone.

i am a victim
even though i don't wanna be one

As the air around us shapeshifted
into light pink hearts
as thick as the fog between 6 & 8
in the morning, his fingers would linger
around my thighs & butt,
lightly demanding me to show him love.

He wanted my hands to roam his earth
rather than us going outside,
soaking in the sun like a sponge
soaking up the water in the sink.

"I just want you to be comfortable,"
he would say whenever I would cry on his bed,
leading into a panic attack,
causing me to wrap myself in a ball
in the corner of his room, hyperventilating
as the room constantly wrapped around me.

A piece of his body contained a sexual need,
which wasn't filled up like wine in a bottle,

& he wanted to get it through me
despite a black & dark blue glass of fear filling me up.

I didn't want to do it,
but he was my boyfriend,
& I wanted to make him happy.

    I thought it was normal.

As the relationship continued
to be something only seen through a telescope,
my body would mix itself in red,
black, & dark blue fruit punch,
wanting me to scream & cry,
wondering why I ever was with him
& why my hands crawled in *every*
speck of his body.

While looking at the black moon
through my white telescope,
its matte black chains
holding me down got looser
like the spine of a thrifted book.

The black air shapeshifted
into light pink hearts,
consuming our lungs,
drowning us as if it was water.
As the relationship began to only be seen

through a telescope,
the light pink hearts subsided,
only to be seen as light pink dust,
& the black air turned into light grey dust,
disappearing into the skies.

his brows & cuts

The silver blade slowly glistened on my fragile skin.
While cutting, a yellow sunflower
slowly started growing inside of me,
feeding on the loss of blood.
But, as I walked out of the bathroom
with hidden bandages slightly tinted red,
the sunflower rapidly died, shrivelling up
as if it had gotten too much sunlight. Then,
while talking to User X,
it was as if a black sunflower
was growing in replacement, causing me to cut again.

His arms were covered in an ocean
filled with cuts, wanting to spill over, desperate
for him to cut again.

As we sat on his grey bed,
he scrolled through the photos on his phone
with a slight smile, &
when the pictures with his arms covered
in blood appeared like an unexpectedly
expected surprise, his smile grew
like a child going through puberty.
Why would he take a photo of that?
And why would he show me?
    I was only his girlfriend.
Was it another tactic to abuse me
                      & get me to stay?

"My mom's worried that if we break up,
I'll kill myself," he said when hanging out.
Was he just trying to get me to stay?
                      Was he lying?

His eyebrows were naturally thick & black,
but the hair on his head was black & thin
as if he was an old man, but it was from him
pulling it out. His eyebrows framed his face

& stood as straight as people in the military.
I wanted those eyebrows.

It was as if he was trying to duplicate
his eyebrows on his arms.

The silver blade slowly glistens on my fragile skin.

slice of life

While we were floating through time,
cutting through the grey clouds
like we were fighting ghastly
monsters in the galaxy, time was arbitrary.

    While floating through the galaxy,

        one day there equalled approximately

        a year & a half.

The galaxy had this special thing
containing time & air. It was like a spell
to keep us under control, like a marionette
who happened to also be a witch.

Our romantic relationship was as if it was controlled
by the marionette witch, & the witch was him.

He envisioned our future together
as if it was just within our reach, ready for us
to reach out.

He imagined what our future would look like,
as if that was what he was living for.
It was as if his lack of good vision was corrupted,
& all he saw were white clouds
telling him what to live for.

He wanted to move outside the country
because it would be better for his "rap career"
than my writing career. *I knew I had to be ready
to make sacrifices, & I figured
that was another sacrifice I had to make.*

                Later that year, I was about to age up
          as if I was a character in a game simulation,
                 & there was this particular air
                      that made my mind think,
why is he more excited for my birthday than me?

As if he was an event planner,
he wanted to hold a surprise birthday party
as if we had been together for four years.
*Why couldn't he give me
                a tangible present instead?*

Cheesecake would be the only thing dancing
around my house as if he didn't know
what else to do or where else to go.

He & I were floating in the galaxy, consumed
in the rainbow waterfall with stars highlighting it.

The relationship was on a thick, white string
as it flopped throughout the night sky,
wishing it was a star, dancing in the sky,
granting wishes for children & giving dreams to adults.

The star would dance in the sky, flying around
as it sparkled its almost invisible dust,
granting wishes to children & dreams to adults
but somehow excluding him
& me as if we were stuck together with super glue.

what is love?

I wanted thick, dark red & pink fur
to cover me like a blanket,
even though I already
had a pink fur blanket consuming me.

the scars

litter my thighs like they're something I gained through simple child's play.

Some days, when thick, black clouds are resting just above my head with rain in the forecast for the rest of the night as I sit somewhere in my house, I think, *Maybe I should add more scars.* Other days, I think, *Maybe they're too much.*

On the days when I think I should litter my thighs with more scars, a tiny itch inside of me thinks, *they don't prove that I'm suicidal enough.* As if, because the majority of them ain't as deep as I would have liked, or as long as I would have imagined, I ain't suffering "as bad."

My arms ain't littered with scars, but the limited scars I *do* have (thanks to 17-year-old me) still sit there, staring at the world, yelling for love, too.

Some days, as I walk through the thick smoke, the scars wish there could be newer & fresher, wanting to party with the older ones.

But when I broke up with my ex, the thick, black clouds faded like the Vancouver weather during the fall & spring. The tiny black twitch roaming my head, urging me to cut, disappeared before reappearing a few months later.

It was as if my mind closed the door & locked it, forcing the black monster & clouds to stay outside.

But then the monster pounded on the doors before kicking it down, overpowering my mind again. The black clouds flooded my mind, implanting themselves within every crevice as the monster swung its veins all around my brain, tightening itself in my residence.

The monster whispers throughout my brain, echoing that *no one would notice if you added one or two extra scars. You should do it. It's winter. No one would notice. You should do it. But then again, no one notices you in general. They wouldn't care if a cut "mysteriously" shows up on your body as if mocking the outside world. You should just do it.*
    Please.

nudes

As our lacklustre love
floated through the air
like a balloon accidentally floating away
from its owner, the completely
exposed silhouette of my body
haunted the Internet but blessed his eyes
as he subtly demanded more
while he said, "I don't want you
to do anything you're not comfortable doing."

As I would attempt to push off
sending him whatever he wanted me to send
as if I was his property, he would say,
"We should talk about this relationship,"
while seemingly constantly
feeling as if we ain't on the same level
     (sexual wise)
whenever I don't wanna give my entire self to him.

As he tried not to have his head blown off
his neck, he would calmly say something like,
"I like you being a tease,

but I would still want some 'action,' too."

It was basically as if it was detrimental to our health
& well-being of our relationship
& would self-destruct within the week
if we didn't talk about the sexual component
(that he so desperately wanted) of our relationship.

> *Less water poured out of my heart*
> *when I did what he wanted*

It was as if I was a sex toy
he bought online in the middle of the night.

> *I knew I had to make sacrifices,*
> *& I thought that was one of them.*

Whenever I would stand in the bathroom
as the white light would shine on me
like a ring light content creators would use,
a piece of me would chip away
like a mountain in the winter.

    That piece would cry like a hungry baby.

Some nights, I would wonder,
does he still have those nudes
                              floating on his phone?
I wouldn't be surprised if he still does.

But I hope he doesn't.

        I wouldn't be surprised if he still stares
            at the photos as my scars peacefully
     litter my thighs as if they were modelling.
           He would already time block
               the following few days
         as if he had always been organized.
He would have his phone in his right hand
              as he lay on his side,
as the white screen would reflect on his face
        like a ball of serotonin. He would grin
            a toothy yet monstrous grin
    as he stared at my body, examining me
    like a female doctor at a yearly checkup.

I wouldn't be surprised
if he posted them somewhere
or showed his friends as he would say,
"Look what I got out of her."
    "What an idiot."
He & his friends would laugh
before talking about music
& their failed-before-started music career.

a sterling silver ring

with a dark purple heart in the middle
sits on the middle finger of my right hand,
& it's accompanied by two rings,
complimenting each other
like a young adult couple
in the honeymoon phase.

Before it began seeing my world
through its prescription glasses,
the purple ring was
labelled "a promise ring,"
as if I had consented to it.

"What do you want as a gift?"

    "You wanna know what I *really* want?"

He nodded.

        "A ring," I said
because I wanted to wear more jewelry,
&, through the process of elimination,

as if I was choosing what post-secondary school
I wanted to attend,
I decided that a ring
was the best choice.

Why did I tell him I wanted a ring?

As we sat at a table at a restaurant
with the ambiance
that a lot of proposals happen there,
he took the already wrapped present
from his coat pocket, handing it to me
as if he was about to propose.

"Maybe I shouldn't have gotten you that ring,"
he said after I joked about how he
"shouldn't have put that ring on my finger,"
with a laugh, thinking,
this is just a ring.
It's not like we talked about,
                                      much less agreed,
on this being a promise ring.
                       He just wanted to know
what present I wanted.

It was as if he thought
he locked me down,
the chains

          t
             u
        m
             b
        l
             i
        n
             g
out from the purple heart,
wrapping around my neck
with a leash he always had.

It was as if that ring confirmed
that I would stay, allowing him
to continue sending me *his* photos
as if I paid for them. *I wanted him
to be happy, & I didn't
want to disappoint (or upset) him
(as if he was a sensitive child),
especially since his eagerness
was the only thing fueling him.*

It was as if that ring confirmed
that I was a doll he had bought
at a thrift store, ready to bend
& move like a marionette.

the midnight moon

I sit at my desk in my bedroom.
                Midnight is in 32 minutes.
My yellow-tinted light
lightly bounces off my light pink wall,
but the darkness still consumes my room.
I crack my knuckles like a baseball player
warming up before his first game of the season
as I look at uPrime videos
on my black monitor while the magical,
galaxy-like river refuses
to leak out for *this* poem.

The uPrime video plays on my monitor
while Scribble is open on my black laptop.

Using three fingers on my right hand,
I swipe right to the left on my mouse pad
& switch to Onyx.
I have to plan content.

A blue river breaks in through my chest,
& every time I breathe, my chest stings.

How am I supposed to be successful?
Why ain't I successful already?
   I yawn.
      I need to read a short story.
I'm wasting time.
      I don't know what I'm doing.

   Midnight is in 29 minutes.

I wish I'm already successful.

I stare at the not-so-blank screen of my laptop.

This poem isn't good enough,
but will it ever be good enough?

The video ends,
& I put a thumbs up to it.

   Midnight is in 27 & a half minutes.

Time warps like metal.

Would anyone even read my story?
Am I even important enough for people to read?

Am I even important?

I lay on my bed with the pink covers
as my laptop charges. Another uPrime video
echoes in the background with Scribble open.
The white screen blasts onto my face,
illuminating the wall behind me.

Who would read a poem about me
                          struggling to write a poem?
My writing ain't good enough.
                    When will it be good enough?

          Should I quit writing?

The monster whispers
in the back of my mind saying,
                    you should just give up
& leave your writing behind.
Your writing ain't good enough.
        You should focus on giving artists a voice,
            connecting readers & writers
& making their dreams come true.

     Is my writing even good enough?
Has my writing gotten better since I was 18?
               Will I ever be good enough?
     Should I give up on this collection?

my thighs

were elastic whenever I sat.
They were also big enough for my ex
to clasp his hand over them
(whenever he wanted)
like he wanted to keep hold
of his prized possession.
                Like someone trying to give a massage,
                      he would rub my thigh,
                        stretching the scars more
                    & subsequently causing a sting
                      to echo throughout my thigh,
                          climbing up to my brain.

We sat in his car in the driveway of his house
in his predominantly white neighbourhood.

I was meeting his parents for the first time.
I should have walked with a gift for them.

It was warm, & hardly any clouds
littered the skies like someone was hunting them,
& they suddenly needed to escape.

I was wearing my favourite dark blue skirt
with a floral pattern
with white, light purple, etc.
flowers covering it.

The neighbourhood was an alternate universe
floating through space
& relaxed like people over summer break.

I was biting my lower lip
as if I was desperate
for blood to stain my lips.

My body was chilly, as if it was winter.

He turned off his car's radio
before turning off the car.

Silence wasn't cutting through the car's air
after I thought that his parents
would despise me because of the scars
dancing around my body.

"They're experts because of me," he said
with a smile as if pleased at the accomplishment.

I should have worn jeans that day.

While we sat on the light grey couch
in the living room, his mother's eyes
would glance at my thighs
as if she was scared that they would jump out
& attack her, too.

It was as if my scars were black monsters
with white eyes, ready to eat her alive.

He inched slightly closer to me,
placing his arm over my thighs
as if that would help to hide them.

As the dark orange sun was setting on the highway,
he drove me home even though I never
            asked.

his marionette doll

I was the doll he could dress up
at the start & end of the day.

He enjoyed dressing the doll
in black leggings & close-fitting shirts.
Then later, he would poke & pry
at its body whenever he
had time to enjoy himself.

It was as if I was dark brown clay
he would form to have
bigger breasts & butt.
He would take photos
of the glistening clay
before placing it in his dresser drawer
that faced his bed.

He wanted me to be a marionette,
wanting me to dance in the air,
floating in the cardboard-filled world,
wanting me to dance for him
& wrap around him

with a pearly-white smile.

It was as if I was his newly renovated house
near the lake close to downtown,
walking in & out of me, desperate
to fix the roof & attic
while wanting to wear wallpaper,
accentuating its hips while hiding
the dimly lit attic & roof
because he would be too ashamed
to showcase them.

But when I broke up with him,
it was as if the clay cracked,
allowing me to jump through the window
in the middle of the night,
dancing & skipping while humming,
"What it's like to be finally happy."

my dream can be

when I was outside with two friends
as the air whipped around us
while we were Downtown
walking in runners
It was early in the evening & we just
came off the bus
with the designer handbags we bought together
the last time we hung out
We laughed like we were in our own movie
The wind continued to dance with us as the city lights
illuminated the streets
sometimes dancing with the moon
We were like ants
as the modern buildings were scattered around us
We walked to the movie theatre
continuing to laugh with wrinkles near our eyes
while people stared at us
as we continued to hang out for the rest of the evening
before busing back to the station
& parting our ways.

he enjoyed

talking about our futures together
as if we were newlyweds,
excitedly talking about our new schedules
for the upcoming week
& what we would have for dinner
later that day.

When we would be in his bed
as he would drift in & out of sleeplessness,
wanting me to do the same,
he would lay in my arms.

"Talking about our future together
helps me fall asleep," he said
one afternoon
as we ignored the dark grey clouds
slowly getting closer & closer to his house.

He wanted to move to Denver
or some other state because
it "was better for [his] rap career,"
as if those States would magically

uplift his beats into something
people *actually* wanted to hear
during their morning shower
or stroll around the block.

Why did the two people even like his music?

His light blue imagination
that would turn black
sometimes would dance in his mind,
bleeding onto me like it was quicksand.

His eyes would softly sit on his face
as his ideal future would be sitting
in front of him as if he was talking to his sister.

Before falling asleep, he would sit
on a light blue cloud &, while dozing off
like a father in the living room,
would imagine what our life would be like together
as if we were about to get married.

counselling notes

- The source of part of my self-doubt & dislike of myself comes from when I was abused. I think.
- *Was I really abused? Was the relationship really abusive?*
    - I don't wanna say I was abused, & it turns out I really wasn't.
- I became suicidal when I was dating my ex.
- I ain't like my box-shaped body.
- How my fingers are too thin & long. I've been told they're piano fingers.
- My face is too long, & when I genuinely smile, it's as if it extends in length like a balloon.
    - I don't like how my face looks when I smile.
- *I wish I was beautiful.*
- Sometimes I think my eyebrows are too thin & curly.
- I hide behind my prescription glasses as if they're sunglasses because they give me a sense of protection from people, as if it keeps them from realizing how ugly I am.
- I think I'm ugly.

his city

was a utopia for families with children & seniors.
His city was a distant noise
from the pollution filling downtown
as if it was in its own bubble like in sci-fi shows.
Apartments didn't run the streets
as if it was a different country,
& it was as if cars were only for show.

The utopia would get caught in the silky,
orange skies as the sun continued to set
over the dark grey & brown buildings.

The park that seemed to sit
in the middle of the city
after exiting the highway
contained natural nature
& expanded farther than anyone could see.

On March 15th, we sat in his car
as the sun danced with the sky.

People walked their dogs.

                        The grass was overgrown.
Lakes held birds.
            There was a gravel parking lot.

Silence was hidden in the backseats of his car.

The sun was still dancing with the summer skies.

His leg shook as if he was close to cracking

the "secret code of life."

"Will you be my girlfriend?"

episode 1: freedom from him

"Everyone in my life leaves me."

                    "I wouldn't leave you," I said
          as if we'd been together for two years,
          && it was the night before our wedding.

"If that poem *is*
about me, then we
should talk about it."

                   It's not like he's the sun.
Did he not trust me?
         Why didn't he believe me?

                        "My poem's about life."

        It was about being in
    a radioactive romantic relationship.

        It was never about him.

"You called me toxic, & it triggered me."

Not even 30 minutes later,
when I video-called him,
he was lying on his bed,
a smug look on his round face.

He thought I was calling to talk about our relationship.

"I'm breaking up with you."

episode 2: freedom from him

He thought he was a thick tree trunk
while I was the light brown vines
wrapped around him.
He thought he was helping.

"*You're* breaking up with *me*?"
"*You're* breaking up with *me*?"
"Why?"

                                          1. Poetry
                                          2. ____
                                          3. ____

It was as if he expected me
to be floating on red & dark pink clouds
amid the morning sky,
expecting me to fall in love
with the beauty of the early morning.

"I'm your biggest fan."

He was chasing a pure white cloud
                        while I was showing my rainbow.

episode 3: freedom from him

"Remember when you attempted to kill yourself,
& we were worried,
& I forgave you right away?"
"I said to forgive me the next time I mess up."

His unanswered words continue to float
in the cyber world, existing as a memory
as his imprint lasts forever.
They aimlessly float around
in hopes of finding their home.

"I miss you."

"I don't know why you broke up with me."

"What did I do wrong?"

"Why are you leaving me?
Can you at least give me a valid reason?"

"I've been so sad for the past week."

"I need you."

"You hurt me so much."

"I just want some closure."

"I'll do anything for you."

"I never felt love like yours."

"You ain't care about me at all?"

"Please answer me."

shelf three

the illusions of talk therapy

I'm doing better, after all. Or maybe it's just an illusion.

the cold night air
dancing in my bedroom

Sunday, November 13th, 2022. 7:46 p.m.

Music plays on my speaker.
The base bounces off the walls.

I sit in front of my laptop
that's connected to my monitor.

I wish my walls were light purple instead.

The moon sparkles in the darkness
with the handful of stars
twinkling in the whispered night.

The sky is as if it was the ceiling of prom.

My hands are like a cold shower.

My arms have dancing goosebumps.

7:49 p.m. Sad rap echoes

& bounces on my walls.

Tears stream down my face
like a missing puzzle piece
trying to find its home.

7:51 p.m. I resume a uPrime video.

I should be reading my Bible.

I should be doing better.

At the back of my mind,
this black goo that continues
to grow like downtown
during the summer. The uPrime video
attempts to beat the goo
like a professional boxer.

The black goo
gets thicker until it bursts
through my hands,
forcing me down & threatening
to cut my arms & legs.

I think I deserve to be alone.

Sunday, November 13th, 2022. 8:01 p.m.

12:11 a.m.

A handful of my classmates
are covered in white & grey.
Some of them bob along
to the upbeat sadness
coated in dark blue,
which blasts through their ears
like a tiger roaring.

Vibrations from the basement echo
into my room
as it sings a dark red lullaby.

A car zooms on the street.
A minute later, sirens follow.
I suck in my breath.
Then, when they disappear, I let it out.

I can't wait to graduate.

When will this week be over?

The darkness the world contains

in its thick shirt sleeves
bleeds out & builds on my chest,
expecting me to handle its weight.
Sometimes the ocean joins in,
thinking it's a game.

      12:30 a.m.

If I'm asleep before 1 a.m.,
I'll have 8 hours of sleep by 9 a.m.,
& I should have enough time
to finish some work
before I nap at noon.

I yawn & rub my eyes.

Counselling's in 6 days.

What should I focus it on?

My stomach knots itself
as if it controls the rest of my body.

      12:36 a.m.

I shouldn't be worrying about this.

         I should be asleep.

1:05 a.m.

on December 5th, 2022. A minute
before my clothes magically disappeared,
I had hit 10,122 words in this manuscript.
It was before the well containing the galaxy dried up.

With closed eyes,
as I listen to uPrime videos
as if they're podcasts,
I hope that I'll be in a dreamless sleep
before it's too late.

I wish I didn't have to sleep.
　　　I wish I could spend all day creating content.
How can I make money?
　　　How can I expand what I'm already doing?
Is my writing good enough?
　　　　　Will it ever be good enough?

being vulnerable

is like being naked with fresh
self-harm cuts on your arms & legs
as you stand in front of the university classroom
in the middle of a heatwave
towards the beginning of the summer
as you give a presentation about economics,
& you're profusely sweating. Your sweat

comes from your forehead &
      s
          l
               o
                    w
                        l
                            y

drips to the side of your face,
& you wipe it away
You can't have people know you're nervous
because you may get points taken away
from your presentation. You ain't a contained,
fiery ball about economics,
but it's better than chemistry.

All I care about is passing this class.

The decider of my grade
sits at the back of the class
with his hands crossed over his chest
as if he's ready to slap
you across your cheek
because you misplaced his favourite red pen.

*I'd rather be dead
than doing this presentation.*

Your classmates stare at you with dark red eyes.

Your hands are sweaty as a pool.

It's like your classmates
can see your heart
& are eagerly waiting
at the edge of their seats to
      rip it out
while you're still alive.

      That's what being vulnerable is like.

how to tell when you're finished pouring yourself into a collection

At the back of your mind
(which seems to be where many
of your liquid emotions hide),
there's an itch that later
transfers to the rest of your body.

What if this really ain't the end?
                    Then I can always edit it later.
What if these poems are trash?
                    Then I can always edit it.

I skim through the list of poems
in my Scribble document
like I'm skimming through my to-do list.

            I'm done.

It doesn't sneak or whisper
in my mind like the black monster.
Instead, it's as if it was already there,

waiting & watching
as my hands flew across the keyboard
as if my brain forced
my fingers to hack into some system
only moments ago.

What if ending this collection
right now is a mistake?
I may be overthinking this.

The itch continues,
but now it dances
& runs through my veins
like a tiger eating its prey.
It itches & then lets out a low growl
until I finally admit that

I am finished.

ABOUT THE WRITER

Angel-Clare Linton is a poet, writer, editor, and publisher. She is also the founder of Spray Paint Magazine.

www.ingramcontent.com/pod-product-compliance
Lightning Source LLC
Chambersburg PA
CBHW031122080526
44587CB00011B/1073